Nurture You

35 Simple Ways to Give Yourself

the

Best Day Ever!

By Harmony Rose West

copyright 2014

Other books in Soul-Full Self-Care Series:

Calm Down!

Get Grounded!

Celebrate Now!

Available at HarmonyRoseWellness.com and Amazon.com

Disclaimer

Copyright 2014

This book is written to help adults and children ground so they can live healthier and happier lives. Although much is shared from the traditions of shamanism, energy medicine, hypnotherapy, meditation, and visualization, the author is not a medical doctor.

None of the information contained herein is to be construed as medical advice. Please consult your doctor as necessary before making any lifestyle changes.

With that disclosed, it is intended that the information contained in this book inspire you to live your life with more calmness, consciousness, presence, grace and ease.

Harmony Rose West

Table of Contents

Disclaimer 3

Introduction 6

What is Soul-Full Self-Care? 8

1. Choo Chew 10
2. The Nose Knows 12
3. Three to Five Minutes 14
4. Criss Cross Applesauce 16
5. Belly Massage 18
6. Hand Massage 20
7. Nourishing Nails 22
8. Pull Your Ears! 24
9. ABRAcadaBRA 26
10. Healing Headache 28
11. Green Strength 30
12. Celtic Weave 32
13. Crown Pull 34
14. Heart Womb Connection 36
15. Hook-up! 38
16. Zip Up! 40
17. Complaining be Gone! 42
18. I Don't Know Moment 44
19. Is That True? 46
20. Cleansing Ball of White Light 48
21. Bless Your Food 52
22. Humming Hummingbird 54
23. I Feel, I Need, I Want 56
24. Sun Love 58
25. A Piece of Inner Peace 60
26. Poly What?! 62
27. The Art of Play 64
28. Expanding Time 66

29.	Flowering Heart	68
30.	A Soothing Blanket of Calmness	70
31.	Anchoring in Self-Worth	72
32.	A Moment of Contentment	74
33.	Give Yourself a Hug!	76
34.	Ease Break	78
35.	Appreciation Rocks!	80
Review		83

Introduction

Too often when we think of nurturing, we imagine nurturing somebody else. A lot of people – your spouse, children, family, and friends – all probably already benefit from your ongoing nurturance, but what about you?

Are you giving yourself any of that good juju?

If you don't take care of yourself, who will? No one else can take care of you in the way that is perfect for you...except you.
This is not to say that we shouldn't nurture each other. We humans are thoughtful mammals who thrive on caring for each other, but the idea that someone else is going to take care of you is ludicrous! YOU are the best person to take care of yourself...to nurture you.

I can just hear you say, "I am just too busy to nurture myself." Though you are busy, would you be willing to entertain this idea of self-nurturance for a moment?

You *can* nurture yourself in your busy life. This self-nurturance takes one minute at a time. Those minutes are cumulative and go a long way towards living the happy and healthy life you know you want and deserve.

~I just want to say **you are beautiful**. Harmony Rose West~

What is Soul-Full Self-Care?

Soul-Full Self-Care is about giving yourself small acts of kindness right now! It's about **intentionally** focusing on acts of self-love.

Soul-Full Self-Care is sustainable, cumulative practices that calm the stress in your body while simultaneously nurturing your spirit.

Soul-Full Self-Care is taking care of your own energy, being responsible for your unconscious habits and changing them so you feel supported in this beautiful life.

Soul-Full Self-Care uses the healing energy of your hands and your thoughts to strengthen you.

Soul-Full Self-Care rituals bring you back to the present moment, this precious now, where all of your power is. It's about being here, instead of there.

Soul-Full Self-Care is taking time to tend to your body, mind, heart, and spirit so that you can walk strongly on your sacred life journey.

1. Choo Chew

Do you have memories of your mom telling you to chew your food-with your mouth closed? Your Mama instinctively knew why those beautiful, strong teeth are so important. Healthy digestion begins in the mouth with the simple act of chewing your food. When you grind those teeth together to masticate your food, your body releases essential digestive enzymes so that it can convert the grain, vegetable, or meat into the energy that you need to grow and thrive. As you are chewing, you also are releasing a lot of saliva which also contains essential digestive enzymes.

Digestion consumes a lot of energy and choo-choo-chewing is an easy, super-simple way to support and nurture your belly!

Sit down to eat breakfast, lunch or dinner. No standing or eating on the run this time.

Take a bite, put down your fork and chew your mouthful of food 100 times...that's right, 100 times! You will notice your food will become liquid, which is what your digestion likes.

Now, you don't need to chew each and every mouthful 100 times, but with each mouthful, do put down your fork to remind yourself to thoroughly chew your food.

Eating with mindfulness will take you longer to eat your food so you may find that you eat less and feel better.

*~A moment of self-compassion can change your entire day. A string of such moments can change the course of your life.
Christopher K. Germer~*

2. The Nose Knows

We live in a culture that is addicted to thinking. With an overload of information coming from every direction, your mind is exhausted taking in and processing this never-ending flood of information.

You have 50,000 to 60,000 thoughts a day. Of these thousands of thoughts, a majority of them are negative, and most are regurgitated. That means that the bulk of the thoughts that fill your head throughout the day are negative thoughts that are repeated over and over and over again. You are swimming in severely polluted waters in the ocean of your own mind.

It's time to become mindful of these thoughts, because only you can have any control over the thoughts you think. Taking a few moments to rest from over-thinking is deep self-nurturance.

Find a comfortable place to sit and take a few cleansing breaths. Close your eyes, and for one minute focus all of your attention onto the tip of your nose. Notice how the air feels on the end of your nose as you inhale and exhale.

If your mind starts to drift back into thinking, gently, without judgment, bring your attention back to the tip of your nose.

As you inhale, affirm, *I am breathing in peace,* and as you exhale declare to yourself, *I am breathing out overwhelm.*

Continue this breathing for a few moments, then carry this focused, nurturing self-care back into your day.

~If you try to comprehend air before breathing it, you will die.
Author Unknown~

3. Three to Five Minutes

When you are in a fight-or-flight response, your sympathetic system is activated. Your heart rate elevates, breathing speeds up, and stress hormones pump through your bloodstream, preparing you to face a threat. If you are being chased by a saber-tooth tiger, this is helpful. If you are stressed because you are upset with your partner, or you have a flat tire, or are late for work, a sympathetic response is not particularly helpful, and in fact, can be harmful.

On the other hand, your parasympathetic system controls your rest, relaxation, and digestion response. When the parasympathetic system is dominant, your breathing slows, your heart rate drops, your blood pressure lowers as the blood vessels relax, and your body is put into a state of calm and healing.

Putting your body in a parasympathetic state is simple if you use your breath. Nurturing breathing exercises have the ability to act as a bridge into those functions of the body of which we generally do not have conscious control.

A great, simple breathing exercise for calming both the nervous system and the overworked mind is a timed breath where the exhale is longer than the inhale.

Sit comfortably. Close your eyes and breathe in and out through your nose.

Inhale for a count of two, hold the breath in for a count of one, exhale gently for a count of four, and finish by holding the breath out for a count of one. Do your best to keep your breathing even and smooth.

Set a timer and breathe this way for three to five minutes.

Revel in the difference you feel in your mood!

~Imagination is the highest kite one can fly. Lauren Bacall~

4. Criss Cross Applesauce

A healthy energy system has energies that easily cross from one side of the body to the other side. This is called being *contralateral*. The opposite of *contralateral* is *homolateral*. Being *homolateral* means that the body's energies are not crossing the vertical midline of the body. This weakens many systems, including the brain.

The energy from the right side of the brain crosses over and is used for the integration of the left side of the body and vice versa. Because of our sedentary lifestyles, most people deeply benefit from intentionally crossing their energies from one side of their body to the other side.

The more you consciously cross the midline of the body, the more your energies will be strengthened, and the stronger and more nurtured your immune system will be.

Stand with both feet grounded and strong. Take a few deep breaths. Bring your right hand over to your left shoulder.

With pressure, push your fingers into your left shoulder muscle, then drag your fingers across to your right hip.

With your left hand, grab your right shoulder. Again, with pressure, push your fingers into your right shoulder muscle, then drag your fingers across to your left hip.

Repeat this crossing-over pattern several more times.

Cross your energies whenever you would like to feel more alert and balanced.
This energy exercise is amazingly simple, yet it's cumulative benefits will help you feel stronger and more nurtured.

~I can do no great things, only small things with great love.
Mother Teresa~

5. Belly Massage

You naturally rub your abdomen when you have a stomach ache, but you can also give yourself a simple abdominal massage when you aren't ailing. It is extremely comforting and nurturing.

You can massage your belly while sitting up, but it is much more relaxing if you lie down. Always massage your belly in a clockwise motion as this follows the workings of your intestines.

You digest food, day in and day out, with hardly a thought about this amazing system of yours. Let's give it some nurturing self-care.

Lie down wherever you can be comfortable. Bring your knees up, and place the bottom of your feet on the bed or floor or put a pillow under your knees. Having your knees in this position helps soften and relax both your belly and back.

With both of your hands, use small circular motions to massage your abdomen. Begin with the lower left part of your belly, right inside your left hip. Massage as deep as comfortable. Keep massaging as you move along the bottom of your abdomen over to the right side, and then up and back around.

Now, stroke one hand after the other around your abdomen in a clockwise direction. Lift one hand over the other in a continuous motion. Increase the size of the circle to cover your whole belly, then gradually make the circle smaller again.

Pay attention to any place that is tender and massage there a bit longer.

Massaging in this way brings circulation and blood flow to your intestines. Even massaging yourself this way for one minute is a valuable way to nurture yourself.

~It is not easy to find happiness in ourselves, and it is not possible to find it elsewhere. Agnes Repplier~

6. Hand Massage

Oh, oh, oh! How many ways, day in and day out, do you use those hard-working hands of yours?

Massage is a wonderful self-care tool. Though getting a massage is a great gift to give yourself, self-massage has its own unique benefits. You can do it anywhere, for any length of time.

A hand massage has at least three awesome payoffs: it increases circulation, helps you have better range of motion, and helps with pain relief from arthritis, carpal tunnel and more. Let's try it...

Start with massaging your left hand. Gently massage each finger, working it from the base of the finger to the tip. Give each finger a little pull. Pinch the ends of each of your fingers.

Put your left hand in your right palm, and using your right thumb, massage your left palm with small circles. Use the fingers of your right hand to massage the top of your left hand as you are massaging the palm with your thumb.

Turn your left palm over, and massage the top of it with your thumb. Deeply massage the web between your thumb and index finger. It always hurts! It is a major acupressure point which is really good for headaches and sinus problems. If it hurts, it means you need to massage it!

Massage your hand for at least one minute, then switch and repeat this massage on your right hand. When you are done, rub both hands together, clap a few times, and shake your hands off. How do those hard-working hands feel now?!

~Courage is the heart's blossom. Author Unknown~

7. Nourishing Nails

Aloe Vera is so widely used that it has gained the name *Queen of All Herbs*. You've probably used Aloe Vera at some point in your life, whether to soothe a sun burn or as an ingredient in your favorite moisturizer. This plant has been used for thousands of years to soothe, nurture and moisturize.

By growing your own Aloe Vera plant at home, you can benefit from it whenever you may need it. It is one of the strongest medicines for digestive issues.

This exercise allows you to enjoy the nurturing, moisturizing properties of your aloe plant while taking time to express gratitude towards your hard-working hands:

With scissors, snip off an inch from one of the Aloe Vera leaves. The thick, succulent liquid will glisten. Rub the cut side over each and every one of your cuticles, saying, *Thank you fingers for your flexibility...thank you for your ease and dexterity...thank you hands...thank you for all you do...for all you share....I appreciate your giving.*

Rub your hands together and soak up all that healing goodness.

~Here is always beneath there. Author Unknown~

8. Pull Your Ears!

The Chinese have used ear reflexology via acupressure and acupuncture for thousands of years to address all kinds of health issues. Ayurvedic medicine has known for centuries that the marma or energy points in your ears connect to your organs and whole body.

Rubbing, pulling, gently twisting, unrolling, and massaging your ears stimulates these energy points. Touching your own ears feels pleasurable since it triggers the release of brain endorphins that help you feel nurtured.

Take a few moments and give your ears a good workout. This is awesome to do before sitting at the computer. Use your fingers to rub and massage every inch of your outer ears. Move towards the center of your ear, massaging all the tricky hard to get at places.

Gently roll and unroll your ear flaps slightly, then massage deeply behind your ears into the ridge that connects your ear to your skull. If you notice some areas of your ears are sore or sensitive to touch, spend a bit more time lightly massaging those places.

Take your earlobes between your thumb and forefinger and lightly pull downwards. Your earlobes are energetically linked to your brain. As you massage the right ear lobe, it allows the left brain and pituitary gland to become stimulated. When you massage the left ear lobe, it allows the right brain and pineal gland to become stimulated, which gives you a whole brain experience.

~When we talk about settling the world's problems, we're barking up the wrong tree. The world is perfect. It's a mess. It has always been a mess. We are not going to change it. Our job is to straighten out our own lives. Joseph Campbell ~

9. ABRAcadaBRA

Many health professionals are now recommending wireless bras since more attention is being paid to the health hazards of having metal on your chest, day in and day out. The wire sits on what in Energy Medicine are called Neurolymphatic Reflex points. Both energy and lymph fluid naturally move through these tissues, but may get blocked due to continual exposure to the wire in your bra.

In a class with Donna Eden, author of *Energy Medicine* and *Energy Medicine for Women*, she educated us that both metal and plastic underwires have the same challenge. They clog energies which need to flow freely and can cause all kinds of health problems. More and more bras are becoming available that are wireless and comfortable. Switch to wearing wireless bras and take tender nurturing care of those beautiful breasts of yours.

If all of your bras have underwires in them, it's time to go shopping for new bras that do NOT have wires in them!

Whether your bra has wires or not, do you need to wear a bra every single minute of the time you are home? That doesn't mean going braless out in public, if you aren't comfortable, but what if after dinner, you took this over-the-shoulder-boulder-holder off and let your energy flow more freely in that area of your body?

Whenever you take any bra off, take 30-60 seconds and massage under your breasts. Put your fingers into a cluster and massage in small circles on the neurolymphatic reflex areas under each breast. Massage under each breast every time you take your bra off. If this area feels tender, don't stop. The tenderness means that you will benefit from this simple nurturing massage.

~Fill what's empty. Empty what's full. Scratch where it itches.
Alice Roosevelt Longsworth~

10. Healing Headache

Self-massage and self-acupressure both bring us into touch with our own healing powers. Many everyday common ailments can be healed by touch. The art of laying on of hands is an ancient way to bring support to any part of the body that is experiencing stress.

Though it is wonderful to get a massage, sometimes self-massage is the best way to affect change. Pressing and massaging specific points on the body can bring energy and blood flow into stagnant areas. Quite often, headaches can be alleviated with simple hand pressure.

Special digestive points, found on the forearms and hands can be massaged easily for the relief of headaches. Massage one hand with the other hand, looking for tender spots while squeezing. Hover on any tender spots, and give a good rub.

One super important point to know about, especially for headaches, is the web of the hand. This is the area between the index finger and the thumb. Find the tender spot in the middle of the web, and press hard for several seconds, while breathing deeply.

Massage this webbing on both hands..

~If you lose your mind, you will come to your senses. Fritz Perls~

11. Green Strength

I am a huge fan of superfoods. Much of our soil is depleted, and food just isn't as nutritious as it once was. Buying organic is the best way to go for sure, yet with all the stress and pollutants that we are exposed to on a daily basis, our immune system benefits greatly from superfoods. Two of my favorite green superfoods are spirulina and chlorella. I often use them together.

Spirulina is so rich in nutrition that it is believed that you could live on it alone for some time! This algae is a complete protein containing all eight essential amino acids. According to David Wolfe, author of **Superfoods**, it is the best source of gamma-linolenic acid (GLA), an essential fatty acid, necessary for a healthy nervous system.

Chlorella contains more chlorophyll per gram than any other plant. It is considered to be a detoxifying food, capable of pulling out all kinds of pollutants from the body. Japanese studies abound touting the healing properties of this amazing plant and its ability to support the functioning and cleansing of the liver. Paul Pitchford, author of **Healing with Whole Foods**, says that the fatty acids in chlorella may be one reason it has been shown to be effective in reducing cholesterol in the body.

Make yourself a green drink!

My favorite recipe is to put coconut water and diluted juice in a glass jar. I then add a teaspoon of spirulina and another of chlorella. This concoction is where I add a few drops of liquid Vitamin D as well as medicinal mushroom tinctures and maca root. I put the lid on and shake well. It tastes better than it sounds and it is sooo nutritious!

Experiment and find something that tastes yummy to you.

~I'm only lost if I'm going someplace in particular. Megan Scribner~

12. Celtic Weave

Your aura is a pulsating, lively sphere of energy that emanates from your body and interacts with the energy of others. It acts like a spacesuit, protecting you and filtering out many of the energies you encounter. It also acts like an antenna, drawing beneficial energies towards you.

This Celtic Weave exercise keeps your aura strong and additionally, keeps the energies within your body crisscrossing over the midline. When these two energy systems are in harmony, your overall health and well-being is strongly nurtured. Any kind of crossover, like crossing your arms or legs, is a variation of the Celtic Weave energy. When you absent-mindedly cross your arms or legs, it often is a sign that you need some repatterning and figure eights to strengthen the Celtic Weave energy system. Let's learn to do the Celtic Weave.

Stand with your hands on your thighs. Breathe slowly and deeply, in through your nose like you are smelling a rose and out through your mouth like you are blowing out a candle.

Bring your arms together into a prayerful position at the center of your chest. Rub your hands together, shake them off, face your palms towards each other, and see if you can feel the energy between them. If you can't, it is not a big deal.

Rub your hands together again, shake them off, and put them up next to your ears, about three inches away, and take a deep breath. Exhale.

Inhale and bring your elbows together. Exhaling, cross your arms and swing them out. Cross them again in front of your body and swing them out again.
Do this again and as you swing out, bend down and cross your arms over the top part of your legs.

Stay bent. Swing out again, in front of your ankles. Bend your knees slightly. Turn your hands towards the front, scooping up that energy. Stand, raise your arms, and pour that energy down over you.

13. Crown Pull

Like I mentioned earlier, the average human thinks 50,000 - 60,000 thoughts a day? (Just how is that measured?!) The majority of those thoughts are negative (*I'm not good enough...she doesn't understand me...there's not enough time in the day*) and regurgitated. That means we are thinking the same crummy thoughts over and over and over again. We are swimming in the caca of our own minds!

When you feel like your head is congested from too much thinking, and you're wishing there was more room in that little noggin of yours, do a crown pull. This nurturing energy exercise also stimulates blood flow to your head, strengthens your memory, and can help alleviate headaches.

You can do a quick ten-second crown pull, or you can take a few minutes and give your head a real treat.

Sit comfortably and take a few breaths. Bring both hands up to your head with your thumbs pointing towards your ears and the fingers of both hands touching. Inhale and as you exhale, pull your fingers down as if your head was a walnut and you were breaking it into two pieces.

Pressure feels good. Pull your fingers down to your ears. Inhale and reposition them on the top of your head a little further back and pull again as you exhale. Keep pulling your fingers apart with each exhale until you get to the nape of your nape. Give a few extra pulls here. Notice how open your head feels!

Now, is it possible to give those negative thoughts the day off?

~Remember to be your own best friend and look within for the source of all Love. Be true to yourself and all else will follow.
Shanta Gabriel~

14. Heart Womb Connection

In this modern age, many women are acting like men as they create through the use of their personality and will. The energy of DOING, of constantly thinking is fueled by the third chakra. Moving predominantly from this energy center is a masculine way to move through accomplishment.

Women who have gestated children know that the true energy of creation lies in the second chakra or womb, not in the third chakra. Though the second chakra is the center which procreates, it is also the birthplace of a woman's innate creativity, and it is here that this creativity is gestated and grown.

Tuning into the fourth chakra (the heartspace) and the energy of love, while simultaneously tuning into the second chakra helps these two energy centers vibrate together and expand the feminine principles of nurturing. It's like giving yourself a giant energetic loving and nurturing hug.

SOUL FULL self care

Standing, sitting or lying down, place one hand over your heart chakra (middle of your chest) and the other hand over your womb chakra (between your navel and your pubic bone). Breathe deeply.

Notice the energies between these two energy centers connect as you stay in this position for one to three minutes.

This energy exercise helps you attune to your natural feminine energies, the energy of nurturing, creativity, and creation. If you choose to, gently affirm:

I join the energies of my heart with my creative center and feel revitalized.

~Love is not a matter of what happens in life. It's a matter of what's happening in your heart. Ken Keyes~

15. Hook-up!

Have you ever been in a perfectly fine mood, enjoying your day, feeling relaxed? Then, you pick up the phone or visit with someone who's all stressed out and flustered, and tune in to find that now you're flustered too?!

In Traditional Chinese Medicine, there are energy pathways called meridians. One runs up the midline of your body through an area known as Central or Conception Vessel. There's another meridian, the Governing Vessel, which runs up the midline of your back. These two energy pathways create your own special container, like an energy egg, wherein your unique energy resides.

When these two energies are strong and connected, you feel strong and connected, and your nervous system feels nurtured and supported. Hook-up next time someone enters into your energy field, and you won't take in their negative vibes.

SOUL FULL selfcare

Begin your day by connecting Central and Governing meridians. It's a great energy exercise to do before you even get out of bed!

Here's how:

Put the middle finger of one hand in your navel and put the other middle finger of the other hand on your third eye (the space in between your two eyes). Lightly push in and pull up while you take a few deep breaths.

You can hook-up throughout your day to nurture your connection with yourself.

~We carry a center that is always returning. Author Unknown~

16. Zip Up!

Meridians are energy flows. Your Central meridian or energy pathway runs up the front midline of your body, and your Governing meridian runs up the back midline of your body. When both of these energies are running forward, you have a feeling of being snug in your own energy and protected from the energy of others and outside influences.

If you don't want to be vulnerable to picking up other people's negative thoughts and energies, Central meridian needs to be strong.

Pulling your hands straight up the Central meridian draws and zips your energy up so you feel more confident and nurtured.

SOUL FULL self care

Let's zip up!

Place your flat palms on your pubic bone at the center of the front of your body.

Take a deep breath as you slowly trace your hands up the front midline of your body like you are zipping up a giant zipper. Zip to your lower lip.

Continuing upward, bring your hands past your lips and raise them into the sky. Exhale.

Bring your hands back to your pubic bone and zip up two more times.

Walk with this nurtured energetic boundary into the rest of your day.

~Daring to set boundaries is about having the courage to love ourselves, even when we risk disappointing others. Brene Brown~...

17. Complaining be Gone!

We were going around the circle sharing a breakthrough we had during the week, when DeeDee told us about her self-imposed daily experiment. "I decided that I was complaining too much." she exclaimed. "I decided that today if I didn't have anything good to say, I wouldn't say anything at all."

"How was that for you?" I wondered, knowing that when I am conscious enough not to bond with others through complaining, it totally changes my experience of my day. "It was truly amazing" DeeDee shared. "I felt like my energy was stronger, and I chose to find other topics to discuss. It was really eye-opening to notice how much we all complain."

In Carolyn Myss' wonderful book. *Why People Don't Heal and How They Can*, she tells how we bound through what she calls woundology: I find something to complain about and bond with you through that wound. It can be something as simple as the weather...*isn't it getting cold...I'm not ready for winter.* How much bonding happens around complaining about our family...*my partner's not doing it right...neither is mine. My kids are a pain...yeah, well listen to this...*

To connect with another person in this way lowers our collective vibration. The bottom line is...it takes two to have a conversation, and we choose what comes out of our mouths. We are the only beings on earth who can speak. As we become conscious of how we use our language, we can intentionally decide to speak powerfully and creatively.

SOUL FULL self care

Today, try an experiment. No complaining, no spending your precious life force whining about anything. If you slip up, commit again. Recommit as many times as you need to. If someone wants to complain to you, decide if you will listen or not, but don't complain back. (Sometimes I put my tongue between my teeth!) If you like the feeling of this experiment, do it again tomorrow and the day after that!

~It's what you learn after you know it all that counts. Author Unknown~

18. I Don't Know Moment

Doesn't there always seem to be too much to read, know, interpret, and figure out? The constant flow of information you need to respond to on a daily basis can too often feel overwhelming.

What if you could take a momentary break from always needing to cleverly figure out the many details of your life?

What if you adopted an I DON'T KNOW position for just a minute or two?

What if having an open mind and not having to know the answer to every single thing could lead to less stress and more curiosity, nurturing and joy?

Let's give it a try, shall we?

SOUL FULL self care

Today, for one or two minutes, when you feel stressed, stop and experiment with the idea that you don't know how to fix this stressful situation. Pretend you've just come here from another planet in the galaxy and you are clueless about life on earth.

For a moment, observe your stress, without judgment. See how neutral you can stay for just a few minutes. See through curious eyes instead of having to figure it all out.

Be aware that not having to know could bring some much-needed relief.

~Sell your cleverness and purchase bewilderment. Rumi~

19. Is That True?

Did you ever see the bumper sticker that proclaims, "Don't believe everything you think?" Most of us have repetitive, over-used negative, regurgitated thoughts, thoughts that are not very powerful and could be called "stinking thinking!"

It's true that we hardly ever question our own thoughts, and oh, the things we think! We think our friend didn't return our phone call because she's irritated with us, when, in reality, her brother-in-law called with an emergency. We think others are smarter than us, can cook better than us, are more together than we are. If we pay attention to the thoughts that are rolling around and around in our mind, we realize that most of our suffering is self-imposed. We create a lot of suffering by believing these unexamined thoughts.

Byron Katie's book, *Loving What Is*, has been a wonderful ally in my life. It has taught me that I am not stuck with my thoughts. No one is thinking them except me. As I have begun to really investigate my thoughts, I realize that with a little focused attention, I can challenge and interrupt a lot of the lies I am telling myself about myself and my world.

SOUL FULL self care

Inspired by Byron Katie, you are hereby challenged! When you catch yourself thinking something unkind about yourself like *(I can't do anything right)*, stop and take a deep breath and ask yourself, "Is that true?" If you answer, yes, ask yourself again. *"Can you positively, beyond a shadow of a doubt know that this is always true? Is it true that you can't...have never...and will never...do anything right?"*

Of course not, will most likely be your answer. *It's not true that I can't do anything right.* Breathe a sigh of relief and tell yourself a more soothing thought like...*I may be having a hard time getting this right, but I will persevere in a kind and gentle way.* By challenging your thoughts, you return to the reality of the present moment while simultaneously nurturing your mind.

~We may regret that we're no longer young, but we're ecstatic that we're no longer clueless. Marianne Williamson~

20. Cleansing Ball of White Light

Our imaginations are a real part of us, yet how many times as a child were you talked out of daydreaming or imagining what life could be like? In our culture, we prize left-brain thinking and value logic. We think it is a waste of time for adults to engage their imaginations, but nothing could be further from the truth.

Suppose that you placed a plank 30 feet long by one foot wide on the floor. Obviously, everyone would be able to walk the length of it without falling off. Now, instead imagine that this plank is placed 200 feet off the ground from one end of a tall building to another. Who then would be capable of walking even a few feet along this narrow path? Before you had taken even two steps, you would begin to tremble, and no matter how much you engaged your will, you would most likely fall to the ground.

Why is it that you would not fall if the plank is on the ground, but you would fall if it were 200 feet off the ground? The answer is that when it is on the ground, you imagine that it is easy to walk on, and when you raise it 200 feet off the ground, you imagine you might fall off.

Emile Coue, a brilliant hypnotherapist who lived in the 1920s, taught that your will is powerless to help you. If you imagine that you cannot do something, it is absolutely impossible for you to do it. Coue teaches, when the will and the imagination are in conflict, it is always the imagination which wins. It behooves us to engage our imagination more than we do. Imagine yourself healed, imagine yourself nurtured, imagine that what you need is coming to you.

SOUL FULL self care

Close your eyes and center yourself. Feel your bottom on your chair, your feet on the floor. Let the inhaling and exhaling of your breath bring your attention to this very moment. Imagine, sense, and perceive a ball of white light sitting on the top of your head. Decide that light has the healing power to calm you while simultaneously nurturing you.

The light is yummy and warm and as you exhale, it flows like melted white chocolate right down into your head. This white light falls down into your neck and your shoulders, then into your torso, filling your arms and fingers.

With every exhalation, you find yourself surrendering to this healing ball of light. You feel it flowing into your hips, down your legs, bathing your knees, and glowing out of your feet. Take as much time as you choose…one minute or a few minutes.

Bring this sense of nurturing and lightness into whatever you are doing.

~Be content with what you have; rejoice in the way things are. When you realize there is nothing lacking, the whole world belongs to you. Lao Tzu~

21. Bless Your Food

Every single one of us needs food for physical sustenance. Yet how many times a day do we unconsciously eat, putting food into our mouths without a thought of where it came from or how deeply nourishing it is? How often do we gulp our food without chewing much and dash off to the next thing?

There are millions of people on the planet who don't have enough to eat. I realize how fortunate I am to have so much food to eat. Almost every time I bring my food scraps out to the compost pile, I think that what I am throwing away could feed someone on the planet. Gratefully, I ask the Earth to take my food offering and transform it into soil that will help grow my garden.

A few weeks ago, my sweet two-year-old granddaughter, Lyla, was spending the weekend with me. As is my habit, I stop before I eat and do what I need to do to bring my awareness into the present moment. Usually, it is a few deep breaths. Since I practice Reiki, I often draw a Reiki symbol with my hand over my food while I say, "Thank you for the food." The first time Lyla saw me do this, she just watched. The next time we sat to eat together, she put her little hand over her food and waved it around, copying what she thought she saw me do. We smiled at each other and Lyla, in her sweet, learning-to-talk little toddler voice mimicked me..."tank oo for food." Gratitude is nurturance we can teach!

SOUL FULL self care

Before you eat your meal, look at the plate of food before you.

In whatever way feels right to you, bless your food. Send some sort of thanks from your heart to your food. Perhaps you say a prayer, or you close your eyes and take a deep breath. Maybe you think of all the people who were involved in getting this nourishment to you, and you thank them. What if you held your hand over your food and blessed it? Blessing your food is a deep way to nurture yourself.

~Rub a dub dub, thanks for the grub, yeah God! A West Family Food Blessing~

22. Humming Hummingbird

The hummingbird's name comes from the vibration of its wings as it hovers or flies through the air. Every time those little birds come close, aren't you captivated by their beauty, their movement, and their hum?

We've all heard the saying, "whistle while you work," but I betcha didn't know that humming while you work helps relax the body's stress response. The vibration of humming creates an internal massage that helps restore health and balance to your entire energetic system. This is a beautiful excuse to find the joy in all we do and to hum that contentment out into the world!

Llama mothers begin humming a few weeks before their babies are born and continue humming through the infancy of their young.

Humming is such beautiful, sweet, nurturing music for both the heart and soul!

SOUL FULL self care

Take two deep clearing breaths.

Now, as you exhale...easily, gently, simply hum.

Don't force it, just find whatever sound wants to flow and let the sound come, gracefully and with ease.

Hummmmmmmmmmmmmmmmmm..............

~Live loud enough in your heart and there is no need to speak.
Author Unknown~

23. I Feel, I Need, I Want

Every single one of us experiences all four core emotions of joy, sadness, anger, and fear. Joy feels wonderful, like getting flowers for no special reason! Yet profound sadness, rage, or fear can stop you in your tracks. You may feel that with everything else that you have to do, you do not have time to deal with strong emotions. The truth is that you benefit greatly by tuning into them and giving yourself what you need.

When I was a young woman, I realized that I often didn't know what I was feeling. One day, I wrote I FEEL, I NEED, I WANT on a piece of paper and hung it on the wall. Throughout the day, I did my best to tune into what I was feeling and what I needed and wanted. It sounds simple, but it wasn't easy. I found I needed that sign's reminder for a very long time!

SOUL FULL self care

Write I FEEL, I NEED, I WANT on a piece of paper, hang it on the wall, or put it somewhere you will see it. For just today, declare out loud what you are feeling.

Start your sentences with "I feel: "I feel angry."
Then go to I Need: "I need to go for a walk or better yet, a run."
Then I Want: "I WANT to feel more peaceful."

Practice I FEEL, I NEED, I WANT for a few weeks, and see if you don't feel more in touch with what you are feeling and what you want and need to feel better.

*~The stuff of our lives doesn't change.
It is we who change in relation to it. Molly Vaas~*

24. Sun Love

For millions of years, humans have evolved under the warmth and love of the sun. In our modern world, we are bombarded with messages about how dangerous this planet is. Perhaps we could benefit from remembering that ancient cultures knew how to use the sun to heal all kinds of illnesses and bring about radiant health.

The sun's ultra violet rays create Vitamin D in the body, which is essential for brain, bone and teeth health, strong immune functioning, and general overall strong well-being and vitality. The sun's light kills bad bacteria and is used to disinfect and heal wounds. Sunlight is known to have a beneficial effect on skin disorders, such as psoriasis, acne, eczema, and fungal infections of the skin.

Sunlight deprivation can result in a health problem known as Seasonal Affective Disorder or SAD, a form of depression. When you sit in an office for the best part of the day, out of the sun, under neon and artificial lights, you are depriving yourself of the illumination of nature. SAD is more common in winter months, but also found in people who work long hours in office buildings.

Let's take a few minutes for some Sun Love!

SOUL FULL selfcare

Don't wear sunscreen or sunglasses. Trust that going outside naked (not totally naked!) for five minutes is good for you, because it is. Now, don't go out in the hottest part of the day and get a sunburn. That's not going to be good for you.

Find a time when the sun isn't blazing, like early morning or late afternoon, and sit for a few moments with your eyes closed, and soak up those healing rays. Thank this glowing planet for its illumination, trusting that it is filling up your battery in very nurturing and healthy ways.

~Try not. Do or do not. Yoda~

25. A Piece of Inner Peace

Every day seems filled to the brim with meals to cook, tubs to clean, and trash to take out. It is vital for you to create a few moments here and there to focus on your inner life. You will never get it all done. Like your internet inbox, the mail keeps coming, and the days keep filling up!

When you stop and take a few moments of inner quiet, your nerves calm down. Your mind quiets, and you connect with your deeper nature. This is self-nurturance at its best.

It is said that a few moments of contemplation, meditation, prayer, or sitting doing nothing is equal to taking a nap.

SOUL FULL self care

Begin this day with a few moments of quiet contemplation. Decide to sit and simply be, before you jump into all your doing.

Wherever you can be alone, sit quietly. For some moms, the easiest place to find privacy is the bathroom!

In the stillness, get in touch with your inner sense of peace, the essential you that exists beyond physicality. As you sit in this meditative state, allow the wisdom of this silence to emerge.

Listening is deep nurturing.

~We carry a center within that is always returning. Author Unknown~

26. Poly What?!

My research revealed that more than 85% of mammals are polyphasic sleepers, meaning that they sleep for short periods throughout the day. Human beings are part of the minority of monophasic sleepers, meaning that our days are divided into two distinct periods, one for sleep and one for wakefulness.

It is not totally clear that monophasic sleeping is the natural sleep pattern of humans. Haven't you noticed that young children and elderly persons nap? It seems that napping is a very important aspect of many cultures.

We, the people of the United States, with our galloping pace of life, appear to be more and more sleep deprived. While naps do not make up for inadequate or poor quality nighttime sleep, a short nap can help to improve your mood, health and well-being.

SOUL FULL self care

Take a nap!

Set the alarm for 20-30 minutes so you don't worry that you will oversleep.

Listen to peaceful music, or let it be silent and soothing.

~When under, remember the surface. When on the surface, remember the deep.

Author Unknown~

27. The Art of Play

I've taught preschool for decades, and I can truthfully say, with sadness in my heart, that PLAY is an endangered species. Elementary curriculum is being watered down and force-fed to young children at a time when they are not mind-dominated. Early childhood is not a time to learn how to add and subtract and regurgitate the names of colors.

Young children are magical beings. They don't live in their minds. Play is their domain, with imagination ruling as they try on new roles, experiment, and just plain muck about. Their products aren't as important as their process. Ever try to hurry a child? They are clear examples of human BEINGS. They occupy the present moment in ways aspiring yogis wish they could!

Most adults value work over play and believe play is a waste of time. Nothing could be further from the truth. We weren't meant to be human DOINGS. Every single one of us is a human BEING. Play is one way to BE who we are without having to perform, think, or produce.

When is the last time you played? How about deciding that today is the day you will give yourself a healthy dose of play?

SOUL FULL self care

How long will you decide to just play? How about starting with half an hour?

During this time you could:

Draw in a journal;

Doodle with your non-dominant hand;

Jump on a trampoline;

Make a collage from magazine clippings;

Dig in the dirt;

Blow bubbles (look online for simple recipes);

Sing;

Dance.

I trust you will come up with the perfect way to play for thirty minutes!

~No bird can fly without opening its wings, and no one can love without exposing their heart. Author Unknown~

28. Expanding Time

Are you running through your days, feeling out of breath and out of time? Are you in a race with time to get everything done? Does your "To Do" list feel longer while the days feel shorter? Is this galloping pace of life supporting you in living the life you want?

Notice that everything that is essential to your life gets done; you eat, you sleep, the food gets cooked, and your family's needs are met. Worrying about what is not getting done can become an unhealthy obsession, one that robs you of precious moments. It has been said that dust can be your best friend. It sits around and waits for you while you are out living!

Some of the items on your list can be put off. Some can be crossed off as not so important. Truly, the most important use of your time is taking time to nurture yourself.

SOUL FULL self care

Set the timer and sit down for ONE MINUTE.

Feel how long and expansive that one minute can be.

Every single thing in life, even time, is a matter of perspective.

Make a decision today that whenever you feel time-deficient, you will stop and feel that time is a matter of perspective, and that there is totally enough time for you to do one minute of self-nurturance.

~The spiritual life is about becoming more at home in your own skin. Parker J. Palmer~

29. Flowering Heart

Who wouldn't agree that flowers are some of the most beautiful creations in nature? They feed insects, birds, and animals, and even provide essential oils and medicines for humans. We revel in the beauty they add to our everyday experience.

Perhaps one of the sweetest reasons to love flowers is that they are given as tokens of love! Take a moment to nurture yourself with a simple token of self-love.

Find a place where you can be still for a few minutes. Calm down your breathing. Feel your heart beating, as you are mindfully aware of this present moment.

Imagine, sense, and perceive a flower seed being planted inside you, above your pubic bone. Plant a seed of a flower you love...perhaps it is a rose, a tulip, or a hibiscus. Let this flower represent nurturing and celebrating the beauty that you are. Decide that it symbolizes the innate beauty deep within your soul...the awesome beauty that is you.

Imagine this seed sprouts into a bud and then it slowly opens as it blossoms and reaches up into your heart. Bring all of your senses into this imagery. See the flower, hear the petals slowly unfolding, and feel the softness of this beautiful creation which is you.

Now, ever so slowly, bend your head down and smell the fragrance of this flower. Breathe in this sweet, simple smell and feel acceptance and love for your innate beauty.

Bring the healing benefits of this nurturing visualization into your day.

~The best and most beautiful things in the world cannot be seen or touched...but are felt in the heart. Helen Keller~

30. A Soothing Blanket of Calmness

Life is fast, and days can get hectic. Having your child fall on the cement can send her into wails of tears. Not getting what he wants can produce a tantrum that would scare a monster. The next thing, you know, the both of you are stressed. If you don't have children, maybe you have your own tantrums!

Haven't you heard "*there is always calm before the storm?*" Like storms in nature, being prepared can help avert disaster. Part of your preparation for meeting the day's waves of emotions can be to develop an intentional focus on calmness that you can call on as you need it.

Bring to mind something that helps you feel calm; perhaps it is music or a beautiful place in nature. As you sense how calm you feel in this special place, let this calmness spread throughout your body. Imagine that a soft, soothing blanket is being placed on your shoulders, melting away any tension, and warming you from the inside out. Rejuvenate in this deep nurturing sense of calm.

SOUL FULL self care

When you are feeling mad, sad or scared, take a deep breath.

Visualize that your soothing blanket of calmness is being draped around your shoulders. Feel how this magical, warm blanket is helping you feel better.

Whenever you need soothing, imagine that you are draping your invisible blankie around your shoulders.

~This night will pass... Then we have work to do...
Everything has to do with loving and not loving. Rumi~

31. Anchoring in Self-Worth

Our culture focuses on the outer part of people, often to the exclusion of
the inner being. Your inner being is the infinite part of you; the part that is pure essence. This is the untouched core of you that lives beyond all of the messages of judgment from the external world. This is the place where you are always enough.

No one can give you worth except you but, most likely, no one ever taught you that. In fact, you might have even been told you had to *earn* your worth. This is absolutely not true! You don't have to *be* or *do* anything to be found worthy.

You *are* worthy, just because you are here. Worth is an inner, innate sense of value which grows as it is tended with nurturing loving-kindness. Make a conscious decision that you will anchor in the truth that you have innate value. Decide to be your own best friend. This one simple act of deeply befriending yourself can propel you towards higher and higher self-worth. Stress won't be able to do anything but take a back seat on the bus of your life.

SOUL FULL self care

Sit quietly for one minute and focus on your breath. On the exhalations, release an untruth you tell yourself about your self-worth. *I am letting go of feeling unworthy....*As you inhale, feel compassion for this inner struggle. *I feel compassion for the struggles of being human*

As you continue to breathe in and out, keep releasing the old untrue message of low self-worth and increasing the compassion you feel towards yourself.

Breathe this way for as long as you choose, and bring this sense of self-worth into the rest of your day.

*~Do not seek any rules or method of worship.
Say whatever your pained heart chooses. Rumi~*

32. A Moment of Contentment

Ah, contentment, what a concept! What if you felt good about each moment of your life? What if you suspended self-judgment and were able to appreciate that each day you are learning and growing? This journey didn't come with a road map. You are creating the map as you navigate this trip.

You are always doing the best you are capable of in any given moment. You know what you know today. Tomorrow you will know more than today. The next day you will know even more. This day is a powerful one. It is the first day of the rest of your Earthwalk journey.

Choose to be content with who and where you are.

Contentment is the best antidote to stress.

SOUL FULL self care

Take a moment and touch your heart. Feel the warmth of your hand as you connect with the love center of your being. Focus on feeling self-love and appreciation for yourself.

Tomorrow is not promised to you. Today is your gift. Choose to feel content for the person you are, and where you are on this journey.

Each moment of contentment leads to another moment of contentment.

Truly all is well.

~Love, and do what thou wilt. Saint Augustine~

33. Give Yourself a Hug!

When I taught preschool, we would have circle time. During this time I would suggest to the children that they hug themselves, and then send love to their moms and dads. As they hugged themselves, their gleeful voices sang, "I love you Mom! I love you Dad!" Oh, how my heart would swell with joy!

It was when I was really wound up that I found that this exercise wasn't just for circle time. I hugged myself as I rocked back and forth. In doing this simple movement, I came to realize the calming, stress-relieving power it had. Perhaps it's why mothers intuitively rock their babies.

I once read that hugging is practically perfect! The only maintenance required is frequent use. Energy consumption is low, while energy yield is high, plus hugging is inflation-proof, theft- proof, non-fattening, non-taxable, non-polluting, and fully returnable! Hugging is natural, organic, non-GMO, intrinsically sweet and 100% wholesome. The best person to hug is anyone, including yourself! The best place to hug is anywhere, including here! The best time to hug is anytime, including now!

SOUL FULL self care

Give yourself a hug! Cross your arms in front of yourself and wrap your fingers around your arms, giving yourself a well-deserved hug. Keep your hands wrapped over your elbows to ensure you are touching the triple warmer meridians and telling your body to calm down its stress response. If it feels right, start to slowly rock back and forth.

Hugging yourself creates a sense of safety that communicates to your body that all is well. Rocking is a surefire way to calm you in the midst of stress and overload. What an easy way to nurture yourself!

~When feeling urgent, you must slow down. Author Unknown~

34. Ease Break

If you are like most people and work an eight hour day, you are on for a grand total of 480 minutes of the day! That is a boatload of time to be working without a conscious break!

What would your day feel like if you scheduled **one whole minute** of ease into each of your hours? One minute...just for you to do something nurturing for yourself. You deserve a break today...a nurturing ease break!

SOUL FULL self care

Decide when you are going to take a break and how you will remind yourself to take it. Perhaps you set the alarm on your phone...maybe you take one at exactly ten o'clock or one exactly at every hour.

During this time, take a minute walk, do some deep breathing, stare out the window, do some stretches, rub your head, doodle...do **one whole minute** of something that brings you some nurturing breathing space and doesn't have anything to do with anyone else.

~The true test of character is not how much we know how to do,
but how we behave when we don't know what to do. John Holt~

35. Appreciation Rocks!

This is the last chapter and it is likely that you were raised to put yourself last like many women were. While it's obvious that you need nurturing, who is going to tend to you? Is it your partner, your mother, your friend or someone else!?

Perhaps you don't have any reliable support resources. Even if you have, the deep truth is that no one will take care of you in the exact way that you need tending to. First, because everyone else is busy trying to take care of themselves! Second, because they are not you.

You are your very best resource for self-nurturing. The greater truth here is that if you never fill your own cup, it will remain empty. You cannot give from lack; you can only truly give from a well-spring of healthy self-care.

Don't you want to experience that self-care and self-nurturance is an essential part of living a healthy life?

SOUL FULL self care

TODAY before you jump into your day, write ten things about yourself that you appreciate, love, admire, respect, adore, and are grateful for.

This is not about anyone else. Just you.

What can you appreciate about yourself, right now this minute?

Appreciation is the best way to nurture yourself!

~In order to experience the magic of life, we must banish the doubt. Carlos Castenada~

SOUL FULL selfcare

Think kind thoughts about yourself often

Greet the sun…feel the wonder of a brand new day

Wear your best clothes,

because this IS the day you've been waiting for

Take slow, deep breaths when you need soothing

Rub your own head, toes, feet, hands, arms…

Walk barefoot as much as possible

Smile because you are alive

Doodle

Light a candle

Hug yourself often

Sit or lie on the earth

Laugh because it feels good

Tell yourself that *all is well*

Wear pajamas for the whole day

Pray for those with less than you

Bathe in gratitude at the end of the day

Go for a walk even though your list isn't done

HarmonyRoseWellness.com

Review

If you feel that this book has added value to the quality of your life, I would love for you to take a few minutes to leave an honest review on Amazon. Your feedback helps others decide if this book will support them in living their best life.

All the best, Harmony Rose West

HarmonyRoseWellness.com

Printed in Great Britain
by Amazon